CW01619664

L

Dark and Light

Published in 2006 by
REAL LIFE PUBLISHING Est. 1995
P.O. Box 74,
Grimsby,
Lincolnshire
DN35 0XA

ISBN No....0 9526422 4 7

Photoprinted and Bound in Great Britain by
Wyndeham gait., Grimsby, N E Lincolnshire.

LOVE
Dark and Light

A book of Verse
by

Sheila Miller

Sheila Miller is a Grimsby born poet with a loyal following from all walks of life. She has been writing in some form or another since the seventies. Her poetry has had several special accreditations particularly from B.B.C. Producers. Sheila is also a lyricist/composer and has written with and been recorded by the world famous singer/writer and film star Charles Aznavour and others. She is a member of Performing Rights and the British Academy of Composers and Songwriters.

Other Publications by Sheila Miller

Pathos Love Comedy
ISBN No.....0 9526422 0 4

Real Life Inside Out
ISBN No.....0 9526422 1 2

Milestones
ISBN No.....0 9526422 2 0

A Walk in Others' Shoes
ISBN No.....0 9526422 3 9

Published by Real Life Publishing Est. 1995

This book is dedicated to my husband David

Words are all I have
But most sincere
No glitter, colour cardboard cut out
Mass production but personal my dear
And words of love do not come cheap
From this mind that never sleeps
But deeper in this heart that keeps
It's silence for too long
You are my love,
You are my poetry, you are my song

Almost all the verse in this book has been written since my last book was published and as I have said previously:-

I try to walk in others' shoes
Understand the way they feel
And then I put my simple views
Of how it seems to me
I cannot touch another's heart
Or get inside their head
Neither can I catch the joy
Or weep the tears they shed
But if I seem to comprehend
In this book for you
The memories, dreams, the sense of fun
Of even just a few
Then I am glad for I'll have done
What I set out to do.

Sheila Miller 1995

CONTENTS

CONTENTS

CONTENTS

THE ROSE

That rose,
The symbol of my one great love
That rose, its autumn petals falling to cascade
On the hallowed ground where our best love was made

We spent and left the truth until tomorrow
Well now it's here
And somewhere some youth is searching in his sorrow
For you and I, who cut our losses long ago
With the rose I gave you just a memory
But it's thorn pierced a life born in secret

Was it real love so long ago? I am not sure
But life has to be respected or it can become infected
And will be no more.

THE RING OF HOPE

She never came home
She said she would
She didn't phone
Had she lied?
Had I misunderstood?

I waited and I waited
Weeks, then months, then years
Inside a ring of hope
Never voicing my worst fears

But the ring of hope
Gave me the scope
To live and so to learn
And I've come a long long way
Awaiting her return

Reality's outside the ring
And I have to say
Deep down and reluctantly
I must step outside some day

RESPONSIBILITY

Thinking it was me had broken up my family
And waiting for those grown ups to return
So I would know when they came home
That God would see how I'd atoned
And a lesson I had learned

But they never came back except one by one
They said it wasn't me but that their feelings had all gone
I ask where I would find them if I could get them back
For losing what's so precious
Gave me anxiety attack

And if they could lose their feelings then I could lose mine
And find that I was wrong and had not loved them all the time
And then I thought maybe, they had not loved me
And so it was my fault
My responsibility.

INSTRUMENT

Let's assume
A single tune could make all children dance
With no variation for need or circumstance
And let's assume there's no room
For those who cannot hear
Or will not dance for sycophants
Who are not what they appear
Who can say how they will play
Those who circumvent
Could it be they'll change the tune
Or the instrument.

THE BEACON *(Love of Humanity)*

They were unaware
They'd sent to me my enemy
And not my friend
And I was unaware how well
I would learn how to pretend
And the aim became to fool the rest
Pool resources for the best
Single minds and thoughts were fused
For the good of the abused
And became a beacon for the free
Shared by my enemy and me.

ONE MAN

I saw the book was covered black
I bought it 'though I wanted white
I read that book from front to back
A tale of one man's lonely fight
To find the truth
With all the facts
And I stayed up all night
Encompassed in one man's resolve
Until I saw the light.

HEROES

Always the winner
You had it all
We could not help but envy you
Succeeding in all that you did

You jumped the fences
Ran the race
Set the targets
Set the pace
And we would be grateful to be placed

Heroes never tell
How they do so much so well
And I often wonder
Are they lonely at the top

I remember now
How we loved you then
Before the cheering stopped

APPLAUSE

Not being athletic
How could I have jumped so many hurdles
How could I
Have crossed the line so many times with no cheers

How could it have seemed I had lost
Only to win, with no one aware of the fight I was in

But if that is so who saved me every time?
Someone loved me enough to see me shine
Who was the locksmith opened the doors
And why did I never hear the applause?

THE PARADE

The sad people had gone home
But the mad people stayed
I did not want to be alone
So I joined the parade

I realised the happiness in madness
Sharing all the daring, the unknown
And wondered the futility in sadness
The virus much more damning
Than the aids when it's full blown

The mad they blew their trumpets
Though their music out of tune
I laughed with them at the inane
Insane, inopportune

The sad would be asleep now
Perusing their nightmares
Afraid to take a leap now
From their troubles and their cares

But me I had it made
At the front of the parade
Blessed, the guest of honour
The best role I'd ever played

BEAUTIFUL

There were no petals on the flowers
No leaves on the trees
But the naked form is beautiful you said
Beautiful and free
Yet unadorned they seemed so sad to me
Then I thought am I like these
Am I what I wear
Am I so sad as the flowers and trees
When I am stripped bare
I run for cover from the lover
Seek the shade
And you dear optimist wait for
The day when I am not afraid
I need my petals and my leaves
I need the colour to cover me
Against a background once so dark
Against the form you see
Beautiful to you
But not beautiful to me.

I HEARD A VOICE

I heard a voice
A voice from the past
It told me the darkness is coming in fast
The voice of the child said
"Give me your hand
Did you forget me
Do you know who I am?"
And I see her way back
Through so many years
And she's so unlike me
She didn't shed tears
She hated the dark
But she didn't cry
She was an island
She never asked why
She did what she must
And she didn't whine
But she was a stranger
And no friend of mine
I could not love her
I did not know how
I could not love her
Not until now
And one night I was sleepless
And I heard her call
I left my bed
And I walked the dark hall
To where she was waiting
That child that was me
I cried as I held her
And we knew we were free.

FACES

I was good at hiding
Amidst putdowns, deriding
I did not care, on the face of it all
And you could not get me behind my wall
But brick by brick I could see it fall
So on the face of it I had to change
The face I'd always known
No more was I out of range
My cover almost blown
So I changed my face cosmetically
So I could hide and they could not see

I am happy today when I look in the glass
But what more will I pay I have to ask
And was it my old face I threw away
Or was it the mask?

THE KEY TO HALF OF ME

All those memories safely in a box
Many may have tried
But no one can break the locks

I keep my memories locked away
So they can do no harm
To bring them out some will say
Will help me be more calm

What do they know
Why I can't go back
The way I came
How can I tell them
The padlock on the box keeps me sane

Why complicate my ordered life
In order to explain
Why the key to half of me
Is where it must remain

DREAM POOR

*I didn't have a dream then
Me I was dream poor
No one ever taught me
That I should want more*

*Concentrating on survival
Plans all locked away
The future seemed to be my rival
Yesterday*

*I could not see a road
Clear for me to take
Never been allowed to
Make my own mistakes*

*And the dream they said I had
It was theirs you see
They could not realise it
So they gave it to me*

*I did it just for them
But no one's ever known
No I never had a dream
Not to call my own*

DEAR FATHER

Oh dear father, not the one in heaven
Dear father how I begged your love
And sometimes I believed you almost heard
It must have been I thought that your hearing was impaired

Now I am grown and you are older, wiser with some means
Famous for your wisdom, bolder with your dreams
You saved up the love I yearned, that is how it seems

But as the torch for you brightly burned in me so long
You fed the world but not this audience of one
Now you play to the gallery and use your precious son
Who will be yours no more, when the audience has gone

DEAR LORD

If I am your instrument
Why did you not make me sharper
So they don't keep on telling me
I can't cut it

THERE'S A KID

There's a kid with a hole in his head
Down in the square
There's a crowd and they're shouting out loud
Come on who dare
They get tough and they love showing off
So the world can hear
As they throw in the boot and they troop
Through the cold night air

The kids are dizzy they roam the city and they fight
And the cops are busy every night

There's a shop with no sign at the top
Gear sold here
There's some kids with a few mouldy quid
For gear, and beer
There's a creep getting fat as a pig
On the kids, do you hear
There's a kid with a hole in his head
In Intensive Care

FRESH AIR

Your life is a country garden
Filled with flowers for honey bees
Mine is a giant window box in the smoke
No room to breathe
In a seething mass
For air, fighting for my share
Hiding that I'm just plain scared
I'll find one day there is none there

DONORS

Tell the donors of my blood
Tell them that it tastes so good
My body's filled with a wondrous feast
And my mind now rests in peace

Tell them I am just a kid
And every single drop they give
I'll justify each day I live

Tell the donors of my blood
I am now out of the wood
And 'Dracula' he once my fate
He is gone and I feel great.

THE COLOUR OF LOVE

He was in care, a cute little fellow
He said "don't call me black sheep
Just call me yellow
Yellow as sunny and sunny for fun
I said "yellow means coward
And you are not one"
O.K. call me green like the grass and the leaves
I said "you're not green for green means naïve
And sadness describes the colour of blue
I don't know why but it just isn't you
He said "there's no colour that I can think of
Is perfect for me but if push comes to shove
What I'd like to be is the colour of love"

WHAT'S IN A NAME

Why marry who you did
For a name for the kid
Trading shame for a name

Kids don't bear grudges
But they see through fudges
Used to hide from judges
Who apportion blame

Besides, what's in a name
If the kid does not fit
And the name it gets changed to
That little shit

I'd lose myself then
Yes, I'd go to ground
Prayed you would not claim me
In the lost and found

Kids don't bear grudges
But grown ups do
And to make my life sense
I've had to condense
My love for you.

JUDGING ME

Judging me would be alright
If you could feel
The pain to which you're blind
The pain that blocks my onward journey
If you could see behind
The mask I wear for you
If you could hear me
Past the silence that we spend
In this home we call pretend
And if judging me would repair
And change confusion and despair
Clear the decks and clear the air
Do it for your self my dear
For I have judged and sentenced me
Although I am still here.

THE LIGHT THAT SHOULD HAVE BEEN

The ones who lost their innocence
Seldom find that spark
The passion of true love
For it was smothered in the dark

Secret days of long ago
And the light that should have been
Can never be a memory,
Can only be a dream

And those who stole that innocence
An oh so precious thing
Could never know the value
Of what they were pillaging

WHO WAS THE CHILD?

He hurt the child he's not excused
But understand the act
When he was a child he too was abused
He's only fighting back
He didn't know what he was doing
He's so full of remorse
And he's so admired by all who knew him
And he didn't use much force
Lock him away? It would turn his mind
Oh it's such a shame
He's taking the pills it's a difficult time
Society's to blame
It's a wicked world, he's done it before
But at least he told the truth
Besides he said he never was caught
Besides he was only a youth
He's turned to God and he's learned to pray
Since people stop and stare
They say "he's an animal, put him away"
It all seems so unfair
He's born to lose, and never to win
Yet he won't bear a grudge
I talked to his family, they stood by him
That did impress the Judge
He's a kindly man so meek and mild
He had the best defender
He never meant to hurt the child
... .Who was the child?... ...
I don't remember

A THOUGHT

If there's no shame

And there's no blame

And Jesus did not

Die in vain

There's one question

Must remain

Why has justice

Such a name?

CHOICES

Kill the baby in the womb
It's not as bad as you assume
No, no more the baby boom
The world you knew is out of tune
Rejoice in choice of yay or nay
Will the baby die today
Will the roulette take or give,
Will the baby get to live
Or did you leave me far too late,
And what will ever compensate.

SCARS

I'd known her for years
When she showed me her scars
The tracks of her tears had long gone
She'd hidden her fears
From her lovers and peers
While floundering then moving on

She'd thought her problems long gone in the past
They could not catch her for she was too fast
But a stumble too many
Stopped her short in her tracks
And she found her thoughts
Move not forward but back

She was surrounded by all she'd cast out
Too feeble to move, too riddled with doubt
She had not noticed for years she was stalked
By yesterday's ghost and the less she had talked
The more she was locked in the cell she had made
Because she was afraid of being afraid

And all she had buried it was exhumed
A bit at a time, a word or a line
A memory awakened a smile or a kiss
An image of love or a boot or a fist
I'd known her for years, her scars had not shown
And I wondered how well I'd hidden my own.

DON'T JUST CALL US FRIENDS

Sisters under the skin
Not even kin
But close as you can get
Blood could not be stronger
Or last longer

Don't just call us friends
It is not enough
It is just a part
For we have shared so much
As if we shared one heart

YOUR HEART

Your heart is in sheltered accommodation
Not an old heart, nor a cold heart
Ticking away never too fast never too slow
Never messed up but never dressed up
With somewhere to go

But it's getting tired of being undesired
Longer than intended
It's a good heart,
Broken now and then
But it's almost mended

As hearts go it's pretty good at giving
And it's champing at the bit
To do some more living

So why don't you vacate
That place you've been of late
Leave a sign moved away there upon the gate
And make another start
For yourself and your heart.

KLEPTOMANIAC

Stealing hearts as if it were your cause
You can't resist taking all to make it yours
And they fall every time for your transparent line

You see it as giving not as taking
Loving and living not as faking

Sometimes you keep them for a rainy day
Or a lonely night for an easy lay
And sometimes you just toss them away

Oh you never think you're bad
When you brag about your swag

And I've seen old skeletons
Dance to your tune and new fools
With old feelings find you appealing

Yet you get confused at who is being used
Because you're so afraid to lose
So you keep on stealing.

I TRIED

I tried to write about you I tried
All I could remember is
He likes eggs boiled not fried
I tried to write how I feel without you
How you charmed my life
I tried to say how proud I was to be your wife
I tried to write it all and tell the nation
But you're just an abbreviation.

YOU OR MY HORSE

You have a personal trainer
So has my horse
You have a rub to make you feel good
So does my horse
To keep in the race you're off like a shot
Pushing so hard to get to the top
So does my horse
But she's faithful and true to who makes her run
And unlike you I am the one
So I'll stick to the filly my wallet reveres
She too costs me plenty but so well she wears
And at least I know her body's all hers.

YOUR LOVE

Your love
The great pretender
The great big spender
In scanties, high heels, long suspender
You, the hero, the tycoon
The gender bender

MAKING LOVE

Making love is like making a cake
You can have the right tools,
The right ingredients
But you need the right heat
Or it will sometimes fall flat

BRIEF ENCOUNTER

So was that it?
Was that why I'm on this earth
Why I risked a heavy girth
Morning sickness, painful birth

Well I wasn't rolling through the surf
I wasn't flying to the moon
In that cupboard in a clinch
I could not move there wasn't room

Would the customers approve
Would they say the earth should move
Shed your clothes and do it nude
And not complain for that is rude

But was that it?
For what I yearned so long

And if I'm scoring up to ten
Should I give you one?
I really do not know
'Cause before I'd come you'd gone

BED AND BORED

Ah, empty vows line the past
And echo with the sounds
Of sighs of love that did not last

For every Valentine you scored
With fiesta dreams
Did not know they could not afford
Any more than bed and bored
With a gallant knight
With no sword.

THE BIRDS AND THE BEES

She's rum
She calls him a bum
'cause he don't bang her drum
But he just keeps mum
He isn't that dumb

He knows…… there's more to come

Oh, it must be a wheeze
For the birds and the bees
When they see you get stung

THE BED

Love was always on the landing
Never lying down but standing
Between dinner and dessert
For the bedroom was for warring
For overeating and for snoring
Not for going off to dreamland
But for going off berserk
With the thought of one so hapless
With a mistress on the mattress
Leaving words inside my mouth
Of condemnation and of hurt
So I gave away the bed
Then it was no more
I said I'd rather have a hammock
Rather kip upon the floor
And the one I gave it to
Was as grateful as can be
It seems that she had been in it
For years more times than me.

REJOICE

There was no erection
Amongst plenty of rejection,
I'd noticed the inflection in your voice
I thought, is it an infection?
But upon inspection
I decided on defection
Now I've seen the resurrection
And its high time to rejoice

MEMORIES OF YOU

I keep my memories of you in a box
A cutlery box
To remind me of the days of spooning
Then the days of always forking out
And finally when we split lives
To remind me you brought out the knives

I try to leave them behind
Each time I move
But every now and then they get used
When I get accused.

CLANDESTINE

I know he likes me he never complains
He eats up my food and nothing remains
Whereas you chase it round and round on your plate
Remind me your mother's cooking is great

I could set the clocks by his visits it's true
I treat him a little better than you
And he comes around when no one can see
Though he's only a fox he appreciates me.

CHIVALRY

Chivalry is dead
I would toss it a black rose
But it's thorns I think may tear
I've prayed for it's survival but I fear
Without it our love
Does not stand a chance

Was it I that killed that charm
That had me thrilled
Made a woman of a simple soul
Did it die on me with my control
Or was it an impostor
And never there at all

Whatever, it was enough
To have me in thrall
I was proud of that skill
Call it what you will
But I should have loved it more,
Kept it fed
Alas, I do believe chivalry is dead.

HAS LOVE LOST THE GAME ?

Running riot
In a love filled with disquiet
Imagination no relation to the real you and me
Truth, once to the fore is no more
But somewhere out there beyond the boundary

And we dodge between the explanations
Like bullets warnings not to see
But look away in case we recognise
Who's the enemy

Has love lost the game
Changed it's name
And now hides in disguise
Would it be better to ask why
Or just believe the lies?

LOVING WILL

Avoiding the void
Searching somewhere, or someone
To break that fall from grace
Out of place in a no man's land
Too lost to find a way
Too weak to stand by
All we planned yesterday

We made each other
Built a giant dream
We wanted the same
And we are not the first fools
To both change the rules and spoil the game.
Where is the loving will to state
If either one finds love almost has gone
Do not resuscitate.

ONE DAY

Though for now I'll have to wait
One day I'll be daft
Like the days when I laughed 'til my sides ached

One day, when I've risen and paid the cost
And accepted life's plans
Can sometimes get lost

I'll go back to that drawing board
And draw me a new life
That I can afford

RING OF TRUTH

Winter and Summer
Had both turned cold
The face of my youth
Now seemed old
My ring of truth
Once sparkling gold
Had turned ....green

ROMEO

Romeo, oh Romeo
Don't treat me like fast food to go
Since your appetite increased
No more am I the all night feast

Fast food can hurt your heart
And some nights when you depart
And you're indulging in some tart
Oh Romeo it isn't smart to upset the applecart

So I must put you on a diet
To appease all my disquiet
For this is war that you are in
And now we're back to rationing.

DIGGING FOR THE TRUTH

My heart is like a garden full of weeds
Once filled with colour but neglected

Someone's been raking,
It's heartbreaking

I'm digging for the truth
For all the seeds that have been sown
In minds not just my own
Now bearing fruit tainted, blown
Since someone's misbehaving

My heart, my garden, my mind will soon be crazy paving

The words I never said are the ones I hear most clear
The song inside my head is the one that brought me here

SUMMER SONG

by Dylan Alexander Miller age 7 years

Summer come
summer go
Summer glisten... summer slow
summer slow
summer slow
summer slow
summer slow
Sun shine ... sun glow
sun glow
sun glow
sun glow
sun glow
Flower bloom
flower grow
flower sparkle... flower show
flower show
flower show
flower show
flower show
Love bloom... love grow

TRAINS

I love trains
Making connections
The chatter of the early morning larks
And counting the sleepers

YOU ARE THAT ROSE

You are that rose
Inspires love when there is none
Passion where desire has gone
You are that prize
To all you mesmerize
And you are mine, most of the time
Yet as to others you appeal
That is when I feel
The thorns of jealousy
Prick my conscience
And I wonder
If this is the kind of love I need.... and if not
Is there a way I can be freed.

A LIFE

They tell me 'get a life'
I've been trying all this time
I've not had that and greedy cat
They say that you have nine
So what's a life to you puss
With so much to spare
When life I cannot suss puss
I cuss but get nowhere

I have been like you
Out there on the streets
And fallen foul as you do
But you land on your feet
I've been battered I've been bruised
With my aspirations flat
But I know now in the next life
I'm going to be a cat

CUPID

Like a sniper with a super dart
You, you pierced my heart

I never did recover

But little did I know
You missed the mark

Your aim was for another

LOOKING BACK

Every time my life's off track
I find myself looking back
To what's left behind
I moved on fast as you do
Hankering something new
Three wives... ... ...
How many lives do you need
To endorse the fact you can succeed

Was it safety in numbers
Was it love as I thought
Or was it always someone else's dream I bought
Anyway, going back makes me yearn
Not to return to today
And the tracks well worn
Since I started to mourn for yesterday.

FIND THE PLANS

There were hard times
Our front door had no knocker
Now we have chimes

But time moves on
Love moves on or moves out
Or carries on in doubt

I've lost my bearings
Since we live beyond our earnings
Lost the plans lost the map
Lost my way must get back

I put a bit away for a rainy day
But you can't save love up
And still get interest

Find the plans
Are we lost
Seek a new route
Whatever the cost

THE PRICE OF LOVE

God was my keeper
When life was cheaper
But some things I could not afford
When prices soared
Well you have to live
And some thing's got to give
So the quarrels with my morals went unsaid
So as to keep my children fed

My heart was the same
My love for them not changed
And I found another name for love
That had to be rearranged
It was a case of inflation
Rising above my station
Moving on before the last
Train had gone.

NO SONNETS FOR ME

You were the poetry, I was your cover
Whilst you were inspired by another
No sonnets for me, just the two line muse
You plotted, I besotted, and abused
Did I know, you may ask, did I feel betrayed
Did I think it was all about getting laid
I don't know - you were heady perfume,
You touched me deep - You - the poetry
I could not keep.

FACES OF L0VE

What is love to me it seems
Is not love to you
For me the years of plenty
You tell me now were empty
And as we fight to prove
The bigger share of anger and of waste
It seems subjective love and even guilt
Can tear down all respect I thought we'd built

I made it easy for you to please me,
But that simplicity
You fell for once in me
Became the silent enemy
What hurts most is not the thought of all that waste
It makes me scared now knowing
Love revered can be two faced.

SHE'S GONE

When you wake she will be gone
The bed her side not laid upon
She's going out to find the sun
She's been the stranger for so long

You'll read her letter stained with tears
Then know her smile's the mask she wears
To hide her loneliness, her fears
Did you no know in all these years?

Did you not see the warning signs?
The silent breakfast morning times
Two souls apart in heart and minds
Could you not read between the lines?

I heard you say, she wasn't tied
She always seemed so satisfied
She loved her home, it was her pride
She loved you too, until it died

You'll read with unsuspecting eyes
Her touching words and realise
We should hear the cage birds cries
Long before she soars and flies

LOVE STRUCK

Exchanging un pleasantries
Yet still in love
With all we had aspired
Even though love
Is sick and tired
The underlying theme ...
The dream
Soaked in sugar
Reality the mugger
Has struck and left unseen

STANDING STILL

I was moving on
You were standing still
Amongst what now had gone
A chasm now to fill
But it filled you with dread
Looking far ahead

You felt in control
In that hole for the dead
With your life delaying
To worship the decaying
And what I should be saying
It remained unsaid

And the further I moved on
The more distant you became
Holding on for so long
You even kept my name.

A WILLING PRISONER

It was her smile first attracted me
A sudden sunburst in a life once drenched with rain
I thought 'wow' that's my freedom down the drain
What an unlikely jailer, and what a willing prisoner I became
No rings, no church, no marriage we were agreed
It should be from want and not from need

Then one night I saw the smile had gone
I was cold, the sunburst had died
I searched for a sign, her eyes were closed
Then I awoke from the dream that had lied
The smile was still there when she opened her eyes
I thought 'wow what a jailer what a clever disguise'

IS IT REALLY YOU ?

Darling it's been thirty years
And my love for you still grows
For I know you're still in there somewhere
'though you've changed your face and nose
I remember still your wrinkles
Every single one
But I cannot find them anymore
For it seems they have all gone
Those laughter lines are buried deep
And you do not smile so much
It seems your face has gone to sleep
'though it's softer to the touch
But your touch my love is just the same
For its just your finger prints remain
You look so young the surgeons say
As they tuck their big fat cheques away
Well for richer and for poorer
And poorer is what I am
I now feel the part
When you call me your old man.

OPEN SPACES

Oh you talk too much
Open your mouth in all the wrong places
I'm becoming agoraphobic
With a fear of open spaces

DEMONS

Sometimes when I'm overwrought
To keep my demons all at bay
To me and them I talk talk talk
'Til they beg me let them go away

AS A CHILD

As a child I would pretend
That my life was at an end
And for the very first time
The stage was mine
And you promised me not jewels
Not a castle for a princess if I lived
But to fill my empty cup with love
And ask me to forgive
The child in me is still here somewhere
But with better dreams to dream
No empty vessel no time to wrestle
With what might have been

I FELT A WOMAN THEN

I loved that womb
That place I carried you 'til you were born
On reflection, I lost it by deception
And even now today its loss I mourn

The man in the white coat
Comforting full of joke
Said 'whilst I'm putting right your pelvic floor
I'll snip it out as you don 't need it anymore

He was nifty with this woman who was fifty
And I did not fight
Well they said the man in the white coat's always right

I miss that womb, I felt a woman then
And that place to me was sacred
Now I feel a certain hatred
For those who call the tunes
And become obsessed with collecting wombs.

STORM

The storm has passed
Yet you still wait for the lightening
It's frightening
What kind of love is it that is restless in the calm?
Why can you not hear that persistent alarm
That tells you 'wake up before it's too late'
Why is it though I have nailed my colours to the mast
You cannot see with me you would be free at last.

But I will wait as I always do
As the next clap of thunder holds you in thrall
And you tell me it's love and for you
Love is all

LOVE AND SEXUALITY

You were gay yesterday
But today you're not
Yesterday you said you loved me
Today you say not a lot
You've chased your sexuality
Like a turkey with no head
Looking for your inner self
You think you'll find in bed
By the crotch or by the dick
Surely there is more
And what if in your search of it
You just find a whore.

DON'T SLAY MY DRAGONS

Don't slay my dragons.
Though you'd sit well in the hero's place
Don't slay my dragons,
Though all you do is in good grace
And I know how brave you want to be
But you can't slay what you can't see
They are inside there is no doubt
You can challenge them to come on out
But it's too late you must let them be
If you slay my dragons, you slay me.

DOES SHE LOVE ME

Does she love me, does she not
Am I happy with my lot
Pick the petals, watch them fall
This I did when I was small
I've lived my life in double Dutch
In the crowd but out of touch
Can a flower tell so much
Does the flower know I'm butch
Will I woo her, will I not
Will I give it all I've got
Or will I rally to the call
Betray myself after all.

CRY WOLF

When do you tell and who do you tell
And if you tell the world will it care
And whose losing face and who will embrace
The truth no other would dare
Who do you ask what would be wise
And who would believe the wolf no more cries

THE FAMILY JEWEL

No debris to clear past the war of words
And all the hot air drifted away
But it's cold and remote as a mountain top
Grubby white flag neither down neither up

I never liked winter, could not stand the cold
Did not think that loving you
Could make me feel old

What a price, with no room to barter
Love the family jewel seems out of date
Will it be reclaimed or thrown away and shamed
Proven to be just another fake.

It's lighting up time here inside my heart
I don't want to lose and I'm afraid of the dark
I'm looking for a sign, just a single spark.

WHAT ARE WE THINKING OF ?

Not knowing what makes you feel good
Or adding up the cost of being misunderstood
I'm not that hot on maths
Subtracting what is bad and past
In this wilderness called love
Looking for a clearing to rest our weary hearts
Cold with the lack of space to let in the sun
What are we thinking of, why don't we just move on.

THE SETTLEMENT

I will keep the dream of the kids we did not have
I'll even keep the burden of how it made you sad
And that remote island that you made for me
Well you can have

You can have the dirty linen
Washed in public and the grease
From the lies I swallowed until they became obese
And our love became a skeleton
May it rest in peace.

THE TWO WHO HAD IT ALL

There was a Christmas tree in every room
With fires burning bright
I suppose we wanted to believe
In the warmth of the firelight
The honesty of love because we were in need
What were we thinking of
Why were we so naïve?

We tried to fill the gaps
With all we thought we lacked
Spent on clothes and gifts and gadgets
Oh how we laughed and laughed
Loud so everyone would hear our happiness
Then drank the lies to sleep
To kill the loneliness

The trees would wilt the New Year fill
With wishes and new dreams
That year would become two
And as crazy as it seems
A bigger home, a bigger garden, a bigger wall
And we would still be known as
The two who had it all

MARRIAGE

If we are a sham as they say
How come I want no other man
And you don't want to play away
What do we have to be to pass the test
I am at a loss to see
What makes a marriage best
No kids - are we selfish as they say
As if we did not try
Don't explain why we remain you and I
O.K. there'll be no replicas of you and me
No little twigs on the family tree
But what the hell, there's still a wondrous tale to tell
Yet they wait for us to fall
Those who must have it all
Who don't see marriage like a tapestry
With colours not all sunny yellow
Not all soft, not all mellow
Sometimes blue, even black
But never too much to lose
And never want it back

CHARITY

You give of yourself such charity
So much so others can be free
And waiting at home lost and alone
Is the hostage to love that hostage is me
I keep on telling myself that I should
Be proud and I am that you do so much good
Still I remain out of the frame
And those to which you play host
I wonder sometimes just the same
Is it they or you whose needs are the most

LOYALTY

Sometimes the price of loyalty
Is too high to pay
And too much to ask, "stay"
But, not being negotiable for you, choosing
Not just a feeling but a calling
Though all of us were falling
All you could see was you had to see it through

I hope they realise, those that were saved
What sacrifice you made
And I hope there will never come a time
When you renegue on what to you
Was a kind of love, a love of justice
And if that is so I should not regret
I had to let you go.

AN OBSERVATION

Pride had a lousy ride
On the wagon of ambition

It took a back seat
Became an island called defeat

And for a while folk would pass
And wave and smile
With the Cheshire cat in tow
Believing that the changing winds
Would never ever blow

SOLD SOUL

You sold your soul for a sum immense
After all those years upon the fence
You hang your head, say you were misled
You were bought in innocence
But with faulty tools it's they the fools
Who cannot make sense
Of the purchase of a soul
Worth no more than twenty pence

THE FAST LANE

You listen to the voice of your ambition
As it leads you down that crowded road,
Too many stops, too many hold ups to the top
And if you fall, who will pick you up?
I, my love, the hostage of your dreams
A prisoner, waiting for the rise
Bracing myself for the faster lanes
Weighing up the losses and the gains
And mounting a search for us
Amongst the sad remains

THE MESSENGER

The messenger is dead
Take your own advice instead
Go back to the start when you had a heart
Before you were spoon fed
But the game is not the same
The rules have changed
You were naïve to believe
Love can be rearranged

I could have told you
And I would have if you'd asked
That greed can change a persons needs
And so the die was cast
Long ago and now my heart
Can never be reclaimed
No more than the love we shared
Can ever be renamed

LOVE IN WAITING

It's alright we can talk
They're too young to understand
And she's so old we can use a code
Just the way we planned

So we have lost the faith
You in yours and I in mine
No point to carry out a search
We'd just be wasting time

They're alright, they've got years
They have theirs to come
And she's alright no stairs to climb
Though her life is almost gone

It's not as if we're doing wrong
By leaving them to carry on
Its not as if we cannot trust
This love that's waiting for too long.

FIRST LOVE

Fashions change
Forever was too long before
The first was the best happiness
Now you want some more

That sweetness on the path
From innocence to sophistication
When what we feel is too good
To be misused misunderstood

First love
Prancing through the daffodils
In spring in search of thrills
Then ignoring what was once no frills
As grass gets greener o'er the hills.

First love
We've travelled far apart too long.
Never listened to our hearts telling us we're wrong.

HOME

Always the traveller,
Was home the beginning of your journey or the end
Was home the enemy or the friend
Was home the haven you would seek
The place I never heard you speak
Out of bounds, relative strangers
Did home lack the polish of that hotel suite
Or the freedom of the forest trek,
The magic of the mountain peak
Was home the unwritten fairy tale
The unread book, the accident
Or was home the You, solitary
Not unforgiving,
Just enthralled in living.

REAL LOVE

Lying to the dying
Painting tomorrow the colour of summer
Though your palette dry
Real love
Knowing when to tell the truth
And knowing when to lie

WHEN

When I'm gone
Between your grieving at my leaving
Will it be long before you hear another song
Smell another's sweet perfume
Let them touch the heart so true to me
That led me to a world of goodness new to me.

When I'm gone,
When you find yourself moving on
I hope the one you choose
Will carry on the work I've done
And you don't lose the scent of me completely
And the ghost of love like ours remains
To roam discreetly.

I NEVER WILL KNOW NOW

Oh the time went by so furious, so fast
The promise of tomorrow,
My obsession as it passed
But tomorrow never came
And as you're not around to ask
I never will know now
If you saved the best for last

NOT TO LET

Her needs
Buried in widows weeds
Doing time for no crime
But in time to be freed
Post the mourning but not yet
With a heart behind the barricade
Marked NOT TO LET.

AS TIME GOES BY

You're good when you die
But things change as time goes by
And all the things you did
Or should have done
Things you're not around to justify
Become the bone of contention
Things that had you lived forever
Would never get a mention
And to think, you, un partnered, unimpressive
Unused to any fuss
Could be the one as time goes on
They all need to discuss.

PARADISE

How will I fit in in paradise
If nobody's lonely and there is no hate
How can I go from what I know
How can I relate

Some have said they loved me dear
I don't understand so I don't hear
Tenderness tears me apart
For I have dyslexia of the heart.

QUICK AND CLEAN

You said "dying slowly is for the holy
I'll choose mine quick and clean"
And that is what you did
I was first upon the scene
But why fly up so close to heaven
And then jump from a plane
Was it the act of the defiant
Or of the insane
Were you so afraid
To wait to die in doubt
Or was it the fear of living
With the lights all out.

AT LAST I'M COMING FIRST

At last
I'm coming first
This is nice this is great
In a life once cursed
I'm loved and talked of fondly
By family and mates
The centre of attention
With no denigration
My speech of thanks long ago rehearsed
At last I'm coming first
The centre of attention
As they place me in the hearse

HINDSIGHT

Being vintage, and knowing
Having harvested whilst the young are sowing
With hindsight being forthright
Little time to shun
So whoever stalks this tiger
Put no bullets in your gun
For you could maim with just a word
Shame with all you know
This philistine absurd
Who understands the status quo.

BURNING WISHES

In my mind
I saw the queue for luck
As hands went up in turn
Then I wished those priceless relics burn

They said the war was over
Wars are never over
Somewhere there's always a war brewing
Always someone disturbing the peace
And the world facing ruin

In my mind
I saw those relics of the rich
Burning in that very ditch
That once had sheltered dying men
I saw those boys I saw me then

And as the flames of my burning wishes died away
I felt so good that I had said
What I know those boys would say
Had they stepped forward as I did
From yesterday

THERE IS A PLACE

There is a place I often muse
Where the innocent win and the guilty lose
Though it hides from me
And it hides from you

One day it will be exposed
For now it's wearing different clothes
Hidden in the murky folds
Are murky hearts and murky souls

There's such a place I've often thought
So fine and true cannot be bought
More sacred that the wars we fought
That never would see us sold short

This place it won't be paved with gold
May be covered up with rust
But shines beneath just like the souls
Of those who fought for us

THE KNAVE

Coward country was not for you
Defending your castle
Like a medieval knight
Not standing for aggression
But standing up for right

It was love in the mix
Of the mortar and the bricks
No regret for the toil and sweat
And so there'd be no flight from the threat
On that perfect summer day

As invaders did their worst
And made their getaway
No white charger, no armour no defence
Just faith in all you'd built
And the Law of Punishments.

LOVE OF PEACE

The wagons are circling
I feel frail
The poisoned darts are hurtling
Beyond the pale
What did I do or what did I not
Is it because of what I have
Or haven't got

Where is the cavalry
Will I be saved
Who amongst the trusted
Now is the knave
So much disquiet
So little calm
But how in the riot
Can they hear the alarm

The buzzards are circling
Appetites obese
I am still waving
The flag of peace

THE BOYS

The boys left so proud
Big smile on the face
In a short while
Men returned in their place

Oh what did they do to the sons that we knew
How can we know what they've seen
In that brief time between boy and man
In the hell where they have just been
Where violence still reigns supreme

Do the guns once a toy
Still explode in their heads
Must we reach for our sons
And find strangers instead

Where are the fragments
Of the hearts of these men
Can we ever put them together again

UNIVERSE

I am the world
You are my lodgers
You move house, move country
Sometimes stay a century

You write poetry
You write beautiful songs
You build palaces, cities
Riches....bombs

I cannot sue you for pollution
Cannot tell you the solution
Too many landlords, it's getting squalid
Breaking all you've built
I can see your buildings disappearing in the silt

Keep me tidy, keep me neat
In all you do and all you seek
For you are just passing through
This Universe unique